Social Intelligence Skills for Law Enforcement Officers

Stephen J. Sampson, Ph.D.
John D. Blakeman, Ed.D.
Robert R. Carkhuff, Ph.D.

HRD Press, Inc. • Amherst • Massachusetts

Published by: HRD Press, Inc.
22 Amherst Road
Amherst, MA 01002
800-822-2801 (U.S. and Canada)
413-253-3488
413-253-3490 (fax)
www.hrdpress.com

ISBN 0-87425-908-8

Production services by Jean Miller
Cover design by Eileen Klockars
Editorial work by Sally M. Farnham

Table of Contents

Acknowledgments

The Social Intelligence Skills model analyzed in this book has been adapted from the Human Resource Development (HRD) model developed by Dr. Robert R. Carkhuff, Chairman of the Board of Directors, Carkhuff Institute of Human Technology.

This HRD model is copyrighted and any use of this material without the written permission of the copyright owner would be a violation.

We gratefully acknowledge the generosity of Dr. Carkhuff for his permission to adapt this material. Two resources provided the major framework for this manual:

- Blakeman, J. D.; Pierce, R. M.; Keeling, T.; and Carkhuff, R. R. *IPC: Interpersonal Communications Skills for Correctional Management.* Amherst, MA: HRD Press, Inc., 1977.

- Blakeman, J. D.; Pierce, R. M.; Keeling, T.; and Carkhuff, R. R. *IPC: Interpersonal Communication Skills for Corrections—A Training Guide.* Amherst, MA: HRD Press, Inc., 1977.

Preface to the Trainee

This is a skills-oriented course: no "should's" or "ought's," but practical, immediately applicable skills. The program is realistic. It is not designed to take issue with the fundamental law enforcement skills you have or will learn in your formalized training, or that you receive from the tutoring of more experienced officers. It is designed to complement both of those: to *add* to your skills base so that when you *choose* to use it, it will be there.

Overview of the Learning Plan

The learning plan is both simple and systematic. First, the trainer will *tell* you what the learning module is all about. Second, he or she will *show* you the skill that will be learned in the module by demonstrating its use. Third, he or she will then have you learn the skill by practicing it in a role-play activity (*doing*). Fourth, and last, you will have *input* into the learning both by evaluating the role player and then having an opportunity to discuss the activity thoroughly, and to give your thoughts and ideas based on your observations of the role play.

Like any training, failure can be programmed as well as success. The key to success is your willingness to participate fully in the written exercises, role plays, discussions, and sufficient practice. Good luck!

Law Enforcement and Conflict Resolution Research

The vast majority of the scientific literature on "conflict management" can be found in the legal and/or organizational research where the emphasis is on the various formal approaches ranging from less formal (such as mediation) to more formal (such as court proceedings). However, a small portion of the research is dedicated to the handling of informal conflict, with an even smaller portion dedicated to conflict encountered by law enforcement personnel in their jobs.

Regardless of whether you search the literature or the internet, and regardless of whether the conflict is in an institutional or personal setting, everyone appears to agree that the most effective ways to handle conflict involves systematic approaches that can be taught. Both the data and common sense support the assertion that being effective at managing conflict is neither instinctual nor by luck or fate, but is mastered via the learning of specific skills related to conflict situations.

RESEARCH FINDINGS

Police using informal approaches to resolve possible conflicts must be keenly aware of how words, body language, and appearance greatly influence community and police relations. Their success depends on being able to translate these factors that influence communication effectively from one side to the other.

Power distance refers to the degree or rank someone has between themselves and others. Low power distance persons prefer collaborative discussion and view subordinate disagreement with and criticism of those in authority as appropriate and desirable. High power distance people prefer authoritarian leadership and dislike disagreement or criticism on the part of subordinates.

When making evaluations of authorities, those with low power distance place more weight on the quality of their treatment by authorities. Those with high power distance values focus more strongly on the favorability of their outcomes; they are not concerned with the subordinate's view. The degree to which those in authority can gain acceptance for themselves and their decisions through providing dignified, respectful treatment is also influenced by the power distance values of the disputants. Informal resolution procedures, such as a warning, are more likely to be effective among those who have low power distance values. Formal resolution approaches such as giving a speeding ticket without being questioned is seen as effective by those with high power distance values.

Law Enforcement Officer Conflict Factors

The amount of conflict law enforcement personnel encounter in the course of their duties is influenced by several factors:

1. The amount of conflict encountered varies according to the nature of the activity being investigated. High anxiety activities (such as high speed pursuits, bomb threats, mob situations, reports of shots fired, armed robbery, requests for urgent back-up) tend to result in increased opportunities for conflict compared to low anxiety activities (such as reports of shoplifting, property damage, loitering, injured animals in public areas).

2. Events attended by two or more officers were more likely to be conflict-evoking compared to events attended by one officer. When two or more officers responded, the situation was more likely to be resolved through the use of confrontation.

3. Events attended by a large number of bystanders resulted in more conflict. However, when the number of bystanders was six or less, arrest was the most preferred solution. As the number of bystanders increased, the use of warnings increased.

4. There is an abundance of research, both field and laboratory, that supports that an officer's nonverbal behavior can escalate or de-escalate a conflict situation.

5. There is research evidence that law enforcement personnel could better manage social conflict if they received self awareness training oriented toward helping them to manage their own emotions, especially anger.

6. When officers are in conflict with another person, and they come to the conclusion that person is disagreeable and emotional, they are more likely to push for a formal process to resolve the dispute (such as a court proceeding) versus a more informal process (such as calming a person down to avoid arresting them).

7. In hostage negotiation situations, systematic and interactional communication techniques are more likely to lead to peaceful conclusions, and role playing is a vital tool in the assessment and training of conflict management/ hostage negotiation skills.

SUMMARY   Lau et al. (2004) found that even brief conflict management training could have significant and sustained effects when training contained the elements of lecture and role play targeted toward increasing participants' self-awareness, strengthening participant's social intelligence skills, and enhancing participants' emotional regulation.

The training in this book addresses the above research factors that increase an officer's ability to resolve and de-escalate conflict with persons they have to manage in their daily activities as officers.

Introduction to the Social Intelligence Skills Model

During this training segment, your trainer will preview the skills model. He or she will explain that the skills to be taught come from the experiences of law enforcement officers just like yourself. He will then outline the model:

INTERVENTION MODEL

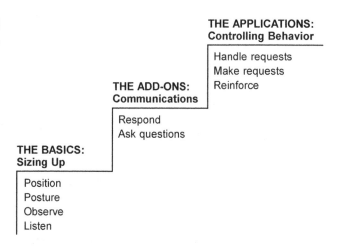

THE APPLICATIONS:
Controlling Behavior

Handle requests
Make requests
Reinforce

THE ADD-ONS:
Communications

Respond
Ask questions

THE BASICS:
Sizing Up

Position
Posture
Observe
Listen

EXPLANATION Traditionally, the training given to law enforcement officers has been aimed at their heads—it was filled with theories and ideas. Sure, there was some skills training, but that was usually in firearms or self-defense. Another thing about the training was that it was almost exclusively concerned with the technical aspects of enforcement. While these are obviously legitimate concerns, this orientation does not take into account the fact that law enforcement officers spend much, if not most, of their time interacting with people—and with each other.

Officers traditionally have been trained to keep the peace, but not necessarily to get along with people effectively. More important, they have not been trained in how to get people to do what the officer wants them to do without a hassle, which is what the job is really all about. This training program is an effort to change that orientation. The program is based on work done by trainers and researchers in the field of criminal justice over the past forty years, and is known as human resource development. It is based on a careful study of the skills that truly effective officers demonstrate. Techniques for identifying these skills have been developed, and now there are techniques for teaching others, like you, how to acquire and use these skills.

This training program is designed around the human resource development model. A model is like a road map: it shows you where you are going. As you can see from the diagram on the previous page, the model has three major sections.

The Basics   **The Basics** are pre-management skills that give you information that helps you decide what action to take in any given situation. Another name for the basics is **sizing-up skills.**

The Add-Ons   **The Add-Ons** are communicating skills that will help you get a person to explore and share information with you. These skills are the key to finding out what is really going on in a situation.

The Applications   **The Applications** are skills that help you control behavior in a respectful way—so that **you** get what you want done with minimal hassles.

During this training program, you will get a chance to learn about and practice all of these skills.

xiv

PRACTICE Think back on your own experience of being supervised. You have probably had bosses who you thought did a good job of managing you, and others who you felt did a poor job. Think about the good bosses. What qualities or skills did they demonstrate that made them effective in managing you—that made them successful in motivating you to do a good job? List those qualities and skills below.

_____

_____

_____

_____

_____

_____

_____

_____

Section I

The Basics: Sizing Up the Situation

The basics are sizing-up skills that help you know what is happening in any situation. Sizing up helps you avoid costly mistakes and maximizes the chances that your decisions and actions will be effective and accurate. Sizing up works because it gets you ready to use information to manage and, often, to prevent problems. Using the basics is always appropriate, because every situation needs to be sized up.

INTERVENTION MODEL

THE BASICS

Sizing Up the Situation

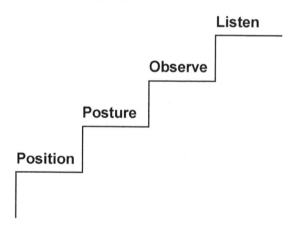

Listen

Observe

Posture

Position

FOUR BASIC SKILLS   Sizing up any situation involves four very basic skills:

1. Positioning
2. Posturing
3. Observing
4. Listening

1

Why basic? The word *basic* is important here. The four skills are basic and fundamental to everything you will learn in Sections II and III of this manual—and to everything that you actually do on the job. You cannot hope to communicate safely and effectively with a person or persons until you have used these skills to size up the situation. You cannot hope to control people unless you have first sized up the situation. By learning to make continual use of the four sizing-up basic skills, you can maximize your chances of making the right response in situations where a wrong response could be very costly.

The four basic skills are cumulative, in that each new skill builds on each previous one. For example, posturing yourself effectively means that you should already be in an effective position, while observing accurately means that you should have already gotten into an effective posture, and so on. In other words, you do not simply use one skill at a time. Instead, you size up a situation by making maximum possible use of all four basic skills.

Getting Ready In general, of course, the skilled officer always systematically sizes things up on his or her shift, whether he/she is responsible for traffic, walking a beat, or being on patrol. Here are some ways an officer sizes things up before actually going on duty:

- Checks with the supervisor and reviews the log book to see what has happened during the last shift

- Reads the log book of the officer he or she is replacing and asks for a briefing about the conditions of the area of responsibility

- Determines if there are items that need priority attention

2

It is in this final phase of pre-duty activity—and in the actual duties that follow—that the officer puts the four basic skills to maximum use.

PRACTICE Why do you think that sizing up the situation is important?

_____

_____

_____

_____

If you were to think about your responsibility prior to going on duty, what would you be thinking about?

_____

_____

_____

_____

Which of the basic skills do you think would be most helpful for you to get that information?

_____

_____

_____

_____

Positioning and Posturing Skills (Nonverbal Communication)

There is no doubt that the development of language has enhanced the growth of knowledge and technology. This growth in knowledge and technology has enabled us to better our quality of life. Verbal and written language has allowed us to pass on to others life wisdom that has increased life expectancy by over thirty percent in this country in the past hundred years.

Despite the power of verbal language, we are more powerfully influenced by nonverbal language in our daily life. Nonverbal language is the way humans communicate, without speaking.

A well-known researcher in this area, whose primary focus was the study of nonverbal communication, postulated the following:

In effective human communication...

- 7% of the meaning comes from the words.

- 38% of the meaning comes from the voice (tone, volume, pitch, etc.)

- 55% of the meaning comes from the facial expressions.

Other research asserts a more modest total for the power of nonverbal communication as being 60% to 70% of the effect on human interaction.

It is also important to note that we can communicate nonverbally beyond voice tone and facial expressions. Following are the eight forms of nonverbal communication that could be utilized by humans in their daily interactions with others.

UNDERSTANDING
NONVERBAL
VARIANCE IN
COMMUNICATION
(60–70% of the
variance)

- Arranging (environmental factors)
  - Physical setting
  - Social rules
  - Cultural factors

- Positioning (body placement; proxemics)
  - Proximity
    Squared/angled/side-by-side/behind
  - Distancing
    Social – 5'-10'
    Personal – 3'-5'
    Intimate – 0'-3'

- Posturing (body erectness; kinesics)
  - Standing/sitting erect
  - Leaning forward

- Gesturing
  - Hands, feet, legs, arm movement

- Paralanguage (voice)
  - Tones/inflection/volume/pauses/accents/
    speed
  - Direct link to emotional state of the speaker

- Facing
  - Eye (movement/contact)
  - Mouth (how one holds their mouth—open/
    closed)
  - Facial muscles (emotional state of person:
    meanings are universal).

- Touching (haptics)
  - Ten times more powerful than verbal
  - Where/how/when is contextually determined
  - Social appropriateness

- Appearance
  - Height/weight/gender/age/race/grooming/
    dress

It is obvious that nonverbal communication is very important and, therefore, must be considered when interacting with others. The relationship of nonverbal communication and conflict is critical for several reasons:

1. We have become so focused on verbal communication due to computers, emails, text messaging, etc. we are probably becoming less aware of what we are doing nonverbally in our daily interactions.

2. Many conflict situations arise due to how one said something (voice tone) versus the actual words.

3. Many conflict situations occur due to inappropriate facial expressions while talking with someone.

4. Many conflict situations occur due to environmental factors such as cultural differences, social roles, and physical setting distractions that draw attention away from those who need our undivided attention.

5. We have become a non-touching culture to the point we do not touch people due to the perception it could be deemed inappropriate, even when it could be very appropriate.

The goal of this next section is to focus on two basic nonverbal skills categories: **Positioning** and **Posturing**. Unfortunately, we cannot address the issues of facial expression, voice tone, touching and appearance. They would require a separate book because of their complexity and their application within a given environment. Regardless, it is important to acknowledge them as critical when engaging others.

Positioning

Positioning means putting yourself in the best possible place to see and hear individuals or groups. This helps you to see and hear what is necessary in order for you to carry out your duties, protect yourself, and to keep minor incidents from becoming major ones.

The three parts of positioning are:

THE BASICS

Sizing Up the Situation

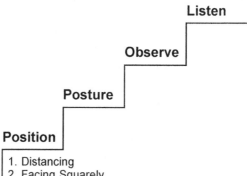

Position
1. Distancing
2. Facing Squarely
3. Looking Directly

Physically positioning yourself in relation to an individual or group is very important in maintaining safety and controlling situations.

There are several different principles or activities that are important to effective positioning. The three basic parts of positioning that we will focus on in this section are establishing an appropriate distance, facing squarely, and looking directly.

As an effective officer, you need to position yourself where you can see and hear problems. Being in a good position helps you to know just what is going on and, therefore, to resolve issues before they become major problems. In addition, positioning helps you deal with people who think that when they are not being observed, they can live by the "We'll get away with as much as we can—or as much as you let us" rule. Of course, it's impossible for you to be everywhere at once. It is also very difficult to catch perpetrators in certain acts because of "look-outs." Yet the more you use positioning skills to see and hear (while patrolling, for example), the less likely it is that people will get involved in things that are against the law.

Positioning also communicates interest to citizens, which gives them a feeling of security, and that you are the protection to which they are entitled.

Now let's look at the three positioning skills or procedures outlined above.

PART 1 OF POSITIONING
Distancing. The first principle of distancing is to keep it safe. Yet while safety is foremost, it is not enough. You could be safely in your cruiser while criminals are doing some pretty negative things. The distance must be safe, but you must also be able to see what is going on. And you must be able to hear what is being said whenever possible.

POSITIONING means distancing yourself
far enough to be safe, yet close enough
to see and hear.

PART 2 OF POSITIONING
Facing squarely. Facing squarely, or fully, ensures that your position gives you the most effective line of vision. Your left shoulder should be lined up with the left boundary line of the area you are watching, and your right shoulder should be lined up with the right boundary line of the area you are watching. When you move your head to either side so that your chin is right above either shoulder, you should be able to see the entire field for which you are responsible.

8

POSITIONING means facing a person, persons, or area squarely.

See Everything

Be Predictably Unpredictable

Sometimes the size of the area for which you are responsible (for example, a section of a community) makes it impossible to remain in one position. In this situation, you must rotate yourself so that by successive movements, you will squarely face all the areas or persons you are responsible for. In rotating, as in all behaviors, it is always important for you to change the order of doing things so that your behavior cannot be predicted easily. Of course, at the same time you must be thorough, regardless of the pattern you employ. Facing fully helps you size up a situation. You can see best when you are directly facing people. When your goal is communication with people (Section II), this also lets them know that you are open to hearing them.

PART 3 OF
POSITIONING

Looking directly. When positioning yourself, you should look directly at the area or person(s) you are managing. Unless you look directly, you will not be on top of the situation, even if you are in the right position and are facing squarely. Looking directly at a group often involves looking at their eyes. When questioning people, for example, you will be able to get important clues by observing their eyes and their facial expression closely.

In addition to the information you can get, your direct look tells people that you mean business and are not threatened. Many people believe that a person who will not look you in the eyes is afraid of you. However, looking directly at someone does not mean you should get involved in a staring contest.

POSITIONING means looking directly at the area and person or people you are managing.

9

Eye contact may also be the best way of communicating interest. People become aware of our efforts to make contact with them when they see us looking directly at their faces. Of course, looking directly at people will also provide you with valuable information about them. People who keep shifting their eyes while talking to you signal that, at the very least, they are either uncomfortable with you or with what is being said. This kind of information is important in law enforcement.

PRACTICE You probably have many duty stations. Think of some of these stations. Describe where you would position yourself to size up the situation.

Station: _____

Position: _____

_____

Station: _____

Position: _____

_____

List two situations in which you think it would be a good idea to look a person directly in the eye.

_____

_____

List two situations in which you think it would *not* be a good idea to look a person directly in the eye.

_____

_____

ROLE-PLAY ACTIVITY

Citizen	Officer	Group
Role plays for 20 seconds.	Positions for 20 seconds.	Critiques officer for appropriateness of his or her position.

10

Posturing

Using good posture means holding your body in a way that shows strength, confidence, interest, and control. When you appear strong and confident, people will believe that you are strong and confident.

THE BASICS

Sizing Up the Situation

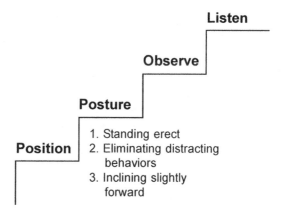

Listen

Observe

Posture

Position

1. Standing erect
2. Eliminating distracting behaviors
3. Inclining slightly forward

Your posture—how you carry yourself—tells people a lot. It can make a person think that you are confident of yourself or that you are really worried about what might happen. Your aim, of course, should be to show your real confidence.

As with positioning, there are several ways in which you can use posturing when you are sizing up the situation. Here we will focus on three specific procedures: standing erect, eliminating distracting behaviors, and inclining yourself forward.

The way in which the first two procedures show confidence should be obvious. When you stand erect and get rid of distracting behaviors, you let people know that you are in full physical control—control not only of your own body, but of the whole situation.

11

And that's essential! Many people (for example, suspects) will try to intimidate any officer who does not look as if he is confident about what he is doing. If a person thinks he can scare you, you are in real trouble. Any officer without respect is open to embarrassment and abuse.

Example For example, there was one officer who was known to run at the first sign of trouble. Other officers felt really uncomfortable with him as a backup. But while the officers did not trust this man, people were always all over him! They always managed to get what they wanted—get him to back down and embarrass him at every turn. Finally he quit. Maybe you would say, "Fine, he shouldn't be an officer!" But his case is just an extreme example of what happens when any officer is easily intimidated—or simply looks as though he could be intimidated.

By standing erect and eliminating distracting habits, you can do a lot to show your strength and confidence.

The third part of the posturing skills outlined here, inclining yourself forward, can also show confidence by reinforcing the idea that all your attention and potential energy is committed to job performance. But inclining yourself forward, as you will see in Section II, can also help you communicate your interest when you choose to provide any human service. Used in this way, such a posture says to an offender (or victim), "I am inclined to listen, to pay attention, to be interested, to help."

All right, let's take a closer look at the three parts of posturing already outlined.

PART 1 OF POSTURING **Standing erect.** We all know how important standing erect is. You probably heard it as a child, and you definitely heard it if you were in the armed services: "Stand your full height," "Be proud, stand up straight," "Stick out that chest," and "Pull in that gut."

12

Standing erect takes muscle tone and practice. Look in the mirror and check yourself out. Are your shoulders straight? Is your chest caved in? How do you feel? Ask someone else for his or her reaction. Which way does he or she experience you as stronger and more confident?

POSTURING means standing erect
to show strength and confidence.

PART 2 OF
POSTURING

Eliminating distracting behaviors. A person who cannot stand steady is seen as being nervous. Biting nails, foot-tapping, and other distracting behaviors do not communicate confidence and control. However, standing stiff like a board doesn't communicate confidence either. A good rule of thumb to avoid stiffness: You should not feel tension in your body after you have eliminated distracting behaviors.

POSTURING means eliminating
all distracting behaviors.

PART 3 OF
POSTURING

Inclining forward. Your intention here must be to communicate interest and concern by shifting your weight forward so that the people become more aware of your "inclination" to communicate and supervise them with respect. You can do this by placing one foot slightly forward of the other with your weight on the forward foot. This communicates "moving closer" without actually moving you much closer or making any physical contact. Since this position shows you to be more alert, it also gives you more control over the situation. Lean your weight away from another person. What do you experience? Probably a "laid-back" sort of remoteness. You are simply not as involved.

13

POSTURING means inclining yourself
forward to show that your attention
is really focused.

PRACTICE List some distracting behaviors that *other officers* sometimes show.

_____

_____

_____

_____

What are some distracting behaviors that *you* sometimes show?

_____

_____

_____

_____

Observing and Listening Skills: Introduction

Nature gave us five senses: *eyes, ears, nose, mouth,* and *skin.* The goal of these senses is to make us aware of our surroundings and what is occurring. We were given eyes to see, ears to listen, a nose to smell, a mouth to taste, and skin to touch. These five senses bring information and experiences into our brain and store them into memory. By storing experiences into memory, we become more intelligent about our surroundings and how we should act to increase our chance of survival.

For example in learning to drive an automobile your senses of seeing and hearing are critical to successfully navigating your vehicle safely. This awareness becomes more efficient and safer by constantly driving while using your eyes and ears and storing into memory what to do and what not to do. This is called experience.

Your lack of awareness due to a lack of experience makes you more accident prone. This is the reason why teenage drivers are more susceptible to accidents. Their lack of sensory awareness due to a lack of experience increases their chances of an accident.

When dealing with people our lack of awareness causes accidents with them that can be just as injurious as a car wreck. A car accident is analogous to conflict.

The more aware you become of people and how you are interacting with them, the less prone you are to conflict or what might be called a social accident.

The other factor in sensory awareness is the "formal" training of your senses to know what to pay attention to. Although we are given eyes and ears that enable us to see and hear, they have to be trained formally as to what to pay attention to.

15

If you were to learn to drive a car on your own, you could learn, but the chances of accidents would significantly increase. By being formally taught what to do and look and listen for through driver education your chances of accidents decrease.

When dealing with people you need to be taught to know what to look and listen for. This should be done formally, not just through trial and error.

These next two modules on **Observation** and **Listening** are just that. You will be taught what to look and listen for when observing people.

Learning these two skills will assist you in avoiding unnecessary conflicts with people, much like paying attention with your eyes and ears prevents automobile accidents.

Observing

Observing is the ability to notice and understand individuals' and groups' appearances, behavior, and environment. Careful observation of actions will tell you most of what you need to know about people, their feelings, and their difficulties. The four steps in observing are:

INTERVENTION
MODEL

THE BASICS

Sizing Up the Situation

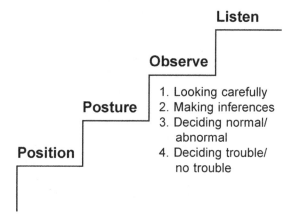

Listen

Observe

Posture
1. Looking carefully
2. Making inferences
3. Deciding normal/ abnormal

Position
4. Deciding trouble/ no trouble

PART 1 OF
OBSERVING **Looking carefully at behavior, appearance, and environment.** A *behavior* is a nonverbal cue provided by something that a person does while conscious and active. For example, an officer might observe any or all of the following behaviors: two people holding hands, one person bumping another, a person looking in a store window.

An *appearance* is a nonverbal cue that a person might display even if he or she were unconscious or dead. For example, an officer might observe the following appearances: one person is African American; another person did not wear clean clothes today; a third person is an older person.

Environment includes the people and things that a person has around him or her in a particular place. When observing a person, you should try to ask yourself questions such as "What's he doing right now?" (behavior), "What are the important things about how she looks?" (appearance), and "What's important about where he is and who he's with?" (environment). Once you are able to answer these questions, you are ready to draw some inferences about a person.

How does she look?

Where is he? And with whom?

OBSERVING means looking at behavior, appearances, and environment.

PART 2 OF OBSERVING

Making inferences about feelings, relationships, energy level, and values. Inferences are the initial conclusions you come to as the result of observing people. You take in visual cues related to a person's appearance, behavior, and environment. These cues are really clues that show you something about a person's feelings, relationships, energy levels, and values. The more observations you make, the more inferences you can draw and the more accurate these inferences will be.

OBSERVING means making inferences about feelings, relationships, energy levels, and values.

Making Inferences about Feelings

The officer can use his or her observing skills to draw inferences about how an individual or an entire group of people is feeling. Knowing how a person is feeling is critical in determining where a person really is. For example, you might use the feeling word *happy* to describe a person who is exercising and smiling. For a person who is pacing while wringing his hands, you might apply the feeling word *tense.* You might use the term *uptight* to describe a group of people who are tightly clustered and speaking with one another in a well-guarded, hesitant manner.

What feeling word would you apply to the following examples?

1. A person is sitting on a bench, head hanging down, slowly rocking back and forth.

Feeling Word: _____

2. In the locker room, an officer is holding up a piece of paper, letter size, while pointing to it and smiling broadly, laughing and occasionally waving the paper around.

Feeling Word: _____

Making Inferences about Relationship

Besides being aware of the nonverbal cues that indicate the feelings of a person, an officer can further increase his or her effectiveness in management by looking for cues that indicate the nature of the relationship between him- or herself and the people he or she works with and supervises, and among people in general. The relationship between the officer, members of the community, and people in general serves as a good indicator of future action.

A person who has a good relationship with an officer may provide him or her with valuable information about potential problems in the community. A person who has a bad relationship with either an officer or another individual may be a source of trouble.

19

Example

Is he positive, negative, or neutral about others?

In general, you can categorize relationships and feelings as positive, negative, or neutral. People who do things to make your job easier (e.g., keep you informed) probably have or want to have a positive relationship with you. A person who always tries to hassle you (e.g., uses abusive language, refuses to obey orders) does not have or does not want to have a positive relationship with you.

Among persons, relationships of power are critical. It is common for people to form their own group with a leader. Knowing the relationship within and between groups is crucial. For example, a bumping between members of different gangs can mean real trouble. In addition, relationships based on drugs, extortion, and gambling are sources of great problems. For example, you might observe that two gang members who have had a close relationship are no longer "hanging" together.

PRACTICE

List two behaviors and/or appearances that would tell you that two persons have a negative relationship:

1. _____

2. _____

What might result from these behaviors and/or appearances?

_____

_____

List two behaviors and/or appearances that would tell you that two persons have a positive relationship:

1. _____

2. _____

20

Making Inferences about Energy Level

High? Low? Medium?

Energy level tells us a great deal about how much and what type of trouble a person can or may cause. For example, people with a low energy level are reluctant to initiate anything. Many people have a low energy level. They look and act defeated. Their movements are slow, their heads hang down, and every movement seems like an effort. These individuals may spend a good part of their time being nonproductive. People with moderate energy levels actively engage in most activities (playing, working, talking, eating), while high-energy people not only participate in all that is required, but also make use of physical fitness programs and many other activities. The danger of high energy, of course, is that this energy needs to be used constructively so that it does not become a source of danger. In general, it is important to keep all people occupied and involved in activities, but with high-energy types, it is absolutely essential.

While it is important to observe basic levels of energy, changes in energy level are even more critical. Energy levels are usually constant for people, except at special times (weekends, special events, holidays). Abrupt changes from high to low to high may indicate trouble (to self or others).

PRACTICE

List two behaviors that show a high energy level:

1. _____

2. _____

List two behaviors that show a low energy level:

1. _____

2. _____

21

List two special times that might cause energy levels to change:

1. _____

2. _____

Inferences about Values

What interests him?

It is also important to understand as much as possible about a person's values. Here is where observing the environment comes in. Every person has three basic environments: the place where he lives, the place where he works, and the place where he learns. In each of these settings, the actual "environment" will include not only physical materials but people—the people who a person "hangs with." You can learn a great deal about a person by carefully observing his environment. A general rule is: What a person gives his energy to is of value to him—the more energy given, the higher the value.

Your observations should help you find out how a person relates to his environment. Does he have girlfriends? Who are they? Remember, birds of a feather definitely do flock together! A guy who hangs out with a drug crowd is telling you something. What are the things that are important for that person? You should look for things in the environment that reflect his interest and values (e.g., neatness, the car he drives). Knowing what a person values has real implications for effective management. When you know what a person wants and does not want, you have an edge in managing that person, when necessary.

PRACTICE

List three things (in relation to environment) that might reflect a person's values:

1. _____

2. _____

3. _____

22

The reasons for your inferences should be **visual cues** related to *behaviors, appearances,* and *environment.* Inferences stand the best chance of being accurate if they are based on detailed and concrete observations rather than on vague and general ones. Inferences are based on your previous observations of behaviors and appearances. The more concrete you can be in describing the appearances and behaviors to yourself and to others with whom you might share them, the more likely it is that your inferences will be correct.

PRACTICE Read the following incident carefully. Be ready to give reasons (descriptions of appearances and behaviors) for some inferences you will be asked to draw.

Incident **November 10, 4:30 p.m.** A group of five large men approached a smallish, young man who was about 5 feet 6 inches, 125 pounds, and surrounded him. One of the larger men put his arm around the young man's neck and shoulder and pulled him abruptly to him while looking directly into his face. The young man grimaced and tried to pull away. The group laughed. After a few minutes the young man gave them something. He then pulled away, head down, barely moving.

Write down the feelings of the young man, his relationship to the group, and his energy level. Cite reasons for your inferences. (The reasons should be descriptions of the appearances and behaviors demonstrated.)

Feeling (angry, scared, happy, sad):

_____

Reason: _____

_____

23

Relationship (positive, negative, neutral):

_____

Reason: _____

_____

Energy Level (high, moderate, low):

_____

Reason: _____

_____

PART 3 OF
OBSERVING
Deciding whether things are normal or abnormal. Once you've been on the job for some time, while observing, you get to know how individuals tend to function. One guy is easy-going and hardly ever hassles you or others. A second guy always looks like he's mad at the world. A third always seems to be feeling sorry for himself. Your observations and the inferences you have drawn can help you determine whether a particular person is in a "normal" or "abnormal" condition at any point in time.

OBSERVING means determining
if things are normal or abnormal.

In determining whether things are normal or abnormal for a person or group at a given time, compare your present observations with any past ones and/or with any comments that other officers may have made about these people. For example, you may observe an individual arguing loudly with another person. He may even be making threats of one kind or another. If this is normal behavior for this person, you probably need to exercise only the usual amount of caution. But if the appearance and behavior of the angry person are highly unusual or abnormal for him, you will know it is a potentially troublesome situation.

24

| OBSERVING: | **Deciding if There Is Trouble or No Trouble.** |
| PART 4 | This decision should be based on your observations and your knowledge of community (street) life. With your knowledge of life in general, you should be able to generate criteria that will be useful in making this decision (e.g., "birds of a feather flock together," "a very depressed person usually withdraws from activities and other people," "when 10 to 15 percent of a group are down, tense, or hostile, it can affect the entire group," "abrupt and/or major changes in behavior and/or appearance means trouble," "a guy who has a history of assaultive behavior has a greater likelihood of future assaultive behavior"). |

OBSERVING means deciding whether it's
a "trouble or no trouble" situation.

For example, take the situation where you observe a problem homosexual with a different partner from the one with whom he had been keeping company. This homosexual's first partner has been acting out, drinking a lot and following the "new couple." Given these observations, you can infer that the first partner is very upset (acting out), has a negative relationship with his old partner (there is a new partner), and has a higher energy level (following the new couple around). You combine these inferences with your knowledge that people may cause problems with other people when a relationship breaks down. You suspect that the first partner is going to try to get even with the new partner for stealing his lover and ruining his image. You decide this is a trouble situation.

Observing appearance and behavior is usually the quickest and most accurate way to detect whether or not a given individual is really having a problem. People may be very reluctant to talk to you about problems. Your observations will allow you to anticipate problems so that you can prepare for their possible impact on other people, you, other officers, or the people themselves. **Remember, nonverbal behavior accounts for 65 percent to 90 percent of any spoken message.**

PRACTICE Your instructor will guide the group through role-playing activities that will give you more practice in using the skill of observing.

1. Feeling: _____

   Reason: _____

   _____

2. Relationship: _____

   Reason: _____

   _____

3. Energy Level: _____

   Reason: _____

   _____

4. What knowledge or principles do you have that would apply to the situation?

   _____

   _____

5. Normal or abnormal? _____

   _____

6. Trouble or no trouble? _____

   _____

Listening

Listening is the ability to hear and understand what people are really saying. Listening helps you hear the signals from people while things are still at the verbal stage so that you can take appropriate action to manage situations before they get out of hand.

THE BASICS

Sizing Up the Situation

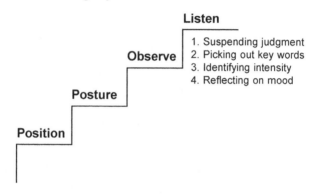

Listen
1. Suspending judgment
2. Picking out key words
3. Identifying intensity
4. Reflecting on mood

Observe

Posture

Position

People often go through a verbal stage before the action begins. If you can hear the signals, you can cut off any trouble before it really begins. Listening involves your ability to hear and accurately recall all the *important* verbal cues used by people—"important" because of implied signals of trouble or problems. The danger may be an individual's intention to get into trouble, harm another person, etc.

Complaints are common, of course, but they are also important. An effective officer listens to complaints and recognizes when a familiar cue is uttered in a new tone, or when a complaint arises from a normally uncomplaining person. An officer listens especially for changes: silence when there is usually noise or noise, when there is usually silence. Once again, the officer asks him- or herself the question: "Is there trouble here?"

GETTING READY TO LISTEN

As discussed, you should get ready for listening by using the basic positioning, posturing, and observing skills whenever possible.

Position

A good position will obviously help you hear better.

Posture

Posturing, while perhaps less important in terms of listening for good management, is essential when you're listening to a person who really wants to talk to you. Your posture can signal to the person that you are focusing all your attention on him or her.

Observe

Finally, your observing skills cannot always be used to promote better listening. For example, you may overhear something that people are talking about around the corner. But when possible, visual observations help you understand the implications of what you are hearing. A person who sounds angry but turns out to be leaning back in his chair and grinning may have only been telling a story to others; an individual whose angry voice fits with his tense, uptight appearance presents quite a different situation.

One more preliminary thing: You cannot listen effectively to people if you have other things on your mind. If you are thinking about home or other job responsibilities, you may miss a lot of what is said and what it really means. You have to focus on the person to whom you are listening—and this takes a good deal of concentration. You can work to develop this kind of concentration by reviewing what you are going to do and who you are going to see before you begin work. Then you will really be ready to start using the four specific procedures that skilled listening involves.

28

Suspend judgment. This is very difficult for anyone to do, but especially for those in law
enforcement. In many circumstances, you have
just witnessed a violation of the law. If, however,
your goal is to get more information about what
happened, you will need to get people to open up
more. Suspending judgment, at least temporarily,
can assist with that.

Still, it is hard at times to listen without immediately judging, because many people with whom
you must deal get defensive (e.g., clam up, get
upset, or become vague) very quickly when you,
as a law enforcement officer, try to talk with them.
Despite this, it will severely hurt your management efforts if you do not suspend judgment
because you will never hear the real verbal cues
you need in order to get more information or to
assist someone.

LISTENING means **suspending your own
judgment** temporarily so that you can
really hear what is being said.

All complaints sound the same after a while,
but they are *not* all the same! Some are just the
normal whines and gripes, while others are real
warning signals of potential problems. Just let the
message sink in before making any decisions
about it. Of course, certain situations call for quick
action, but if you develop your nonjudgmental listening ability, you will hear better and be able to
take appropriate action more quickly, when
necessary.

Pick out key words. There are key words and
phrases to listen for. Here are a few: *kill,
depressed, snitch, honky, waste, hawk, staff.* Of
course, everything you hear and see must be
considered in terms of who did or said it. Some
people are always sounding off. In addition to the

29

key words you hear, it's important to add your observations and knowledge of the person who said them.

LISTENING means **picking out the key phrases** such as *get* or *piece* or *that S.O.B.*

PRACTICE   List some words and phrases that signal danger or trouble in your particular environment.

PART 3 OF
LISTENING

Volume?
Emotion?
Intensity?
High, medium,
low?

Identify intensity. Statements are made with varying intensity (high, moderate, and low). The louder and more emotional a statement, the more intense it is. But loudness and emotion are not the same thing. A wavering voice, for example, signals a lot of emotion, even though it may not be loud. A statement that is either loud or emotional but not both is most often of moderate intensity.

A statement that is loud and is empty of emotion is usually of low intensity. High intensity statements are very real signs of danger.

LISTENING means **determining whether the intensity of a person's speech is high, medium, or low.**

PART 4 OF
LISTENING

Reflect on what the mood is. Is the person's mood positive, negative, or neutral? Normal or abnormal? Why? *Mood* here means, at a very simple level, what people are feeling. One question you may ask to determine mood is "What kinds of feelings are being expressed or implied (positive, negative, or neutral)?"

Another question you want to answer is "Is this mood normal or abnormal for this time and place?" Sure, there are always exceptions. For example, a person can say "I'm going to kill you" quietly and without emotion, yet still mean it. This is why it is so important to know as much as possible and to continue to observe and listen for other cues.

LISTENING means **determining whether a mood is positive, neutral, or negative,** and whether this mood is normal or abnormal.

Reasons When you answer the question, "Is this normal or abnormal?" you should try to formulate the reason why this is the case. *Normal* means "as it usually is." This can apply to an individual as well as to a large group of people. People are usually quite consistent in their behaviors in their various settings—they are creatures of habit. For example, it is not normal for people to be real quiet when they are among others who are being very noisy and animated.

31

ROLE-PLAY ACTIVITY

Person	Officer	Group
1) Describes setting. **2)** Role plays person for 20 to 30 seconds. **3)** Provides verbal cues for conveying information (high, medium, low). **4)** Defines mood (positive, negative, neutral). **5)** Determines mood (normal, abnormal). **6)** Why?	**1)** Positions Postures Observes Suspends judgment Says nothing **2)** Pulls out key words. **3)** Identifies intensity. **4)** Rates person on #2 through #6 (yes/no).	**1)** Positions for paying attention. **2)** Writes own answer. **3)** Rates officer on sizing-up skills.

It was not that long since Harry had finished his training and gone on his beat. But his lack of experience really didn't bother him too much. He had a lot going for him. For one thing, he had some good basic skills.

He walked around the park making observations. On one bench two older fellows talked softly—their usual behavior. He had watched them before. They would talk for an hour—no more, no less. All part of their own little routine. No problems. In another place a young guy lay on his back in a grassy area. A guy near him, an older man, paced back and forth. Tension there, one guy lying quietly, another appearing pretty nervous.

"How's it going?" Harry stopped three or four feet from the older man who turned so that Harry faced him squarely, and at the same time could easily observe the younger guy on the ground. "Is that your buddy there on the grass?" "Yeah, he's not feeling so good, so he's getting a snooze in."

The older man nodded and went back to pacing. Harry turned slightly to get closer to the young guy. Since the older guy still seemed nervous, Harry positioned himself so that he could keep him in view while he sized up the younger man.

Upon closer observation, he noticed saliva oozing from the corner of the younger guy's mouth. His lips appeared bluish and he noticed that his respiration appeared shallow and erratic. He immediately put in a call for backup and for an emergency medical response. This guy is not snoozing, he is not functioning normally.

Harry has a lot going for him with his basic skills, and now you have the same skills working for you. Being able to size things up means being able to minimize risk and maximize your effectiveness on the job. Being a law enforcement officer is never easy, but it is almost impossible if all you have to go on is impulse and habit! Now you can move beyond these limited capabilities and start to put some real professionalism into your work.

You have had a chance to learn the four basic skills you need to size up a situation—to manage your job and people more effectively. You have practiced positioning, posturing, observing, and listening. But as you know, there is far more to being an effective officer than being able to size things up. There will be times when you choose to manage by communicating. You will want to defuse a troublesome situation or get important information. There may even be times you choose to become more involved.

In the second major section of this manual, we will consider the skills you will need to communicate effectively. The skills in this section, while often secondary to other management skills in some situations, are absolutely essential when dealing with many tense situations—situations where strong feelings may get out of control or are interfering with your ability to understand what you need to. Sizing things up just lets you know what is happening and what may happen. To manage things for the better—and that is what effective management requires—you need to add on communication skills.

THE ADD-ONS

Communicating
with People

THE BASICS

Sizing Up
the Situation

Section II

Verbal Communication

We are a talking species—we value language and the use of words. We are taught at a very early age to hear, speak, read, and write words. We use them to communicate our thoughts, feelings, and needs. A major component of human intelligence is based on a person's vocabulary. In other words, we tend to judge how intelligent a person is based on how large their vocabulary is. The bottom line is that when we talk to people, we use words. Unfortunately, having a broad vocabulary does not ensure social success in human interactions.

Besides words themselves, there are verbal techniques necessary to accomplish your relationship goals. A verbal technique is how to say something beyond the words themselves. An analogy would be the throwing of a baseball or softball using a certain technique when you release the ball. The pitcher cradles the ball in his or her hand in different ways such that, when the ball is thrown, it follows different paths (e.g., fast ball, change up, curve ball). These different paths, or the delivery of the ball, represent the technique.

When we talk with others, the techniques, as well as the words, are critical in determining the outcome. In these next two sections we will focus on two verbal techniques: The **Add-On** Skills and the **Application** Skills.

The **Add-On** skills are communication skills that emphasize building rapport with people. The building of rapport is critical because when there is rapport there is less conflict potential.

The second set of skills are the **Application** skills, sometimes referred to as the **Managing** skills. These application skills are the cornerstone of law enforcement, because they emphasize "managing" the behaviors of others. Managing the behavior of others is what you do.

The application skills are presented in the last phase of the book, because your ability to manage others with less conflict requires being skilled in the **Basic** and **Add-On** skills. Let us discuss the **Add-On** skills.

The Add-Ons:
Communicating with People

Add-on skills help you open up communication with people. They provide you with the ability to get another person to tell you more about what he or she knows or thinks. You will find the add-on communicating skills invaluable whenever you need to get more information about a situation, or when you **choose** to become involved.

The two add-on communicating skills are:

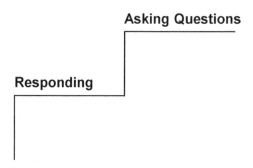

THE ADD-ONS

Communicating with People

Asking Questions

Responding

It has been said that the only thing worse than a young person who thinks he or she knows it all is an older person who is sure he or she knows it all—but does not. You may be new to law enforcement, or you may have some level of experience, but whatever your situation you have probably run across officers who are very rigid in their approach. They see little need for juries or judges. To these officers, anything less than "throwing the book" at someone is weak and the reason the system does not work. There is a lot of logic in their thinking, but only up to a point.

One older officer found this out to his considerable embarrassment. A new, young officer recently started work and was cheerful enough, but did not say much. But then again, what would a man with only a few month's experience have to say anyway? Even so, the experienced man figured him for an academy whiz kid who thought he had all the answers. He did not.

One day the two happened to be on duty together. A street character named Larry got the older man aside and tipped him off about some drugs that Jess, another transient, had stashed. Minutes later, the experienced officer had Jess and was conducting a thorough search of the "room" he slept in. Sure enough, they found a small amount of drugs hidden in his bedding.

"That's kind of hard to believe," the young officer said to the older officer once Jess had been written up.

"Yea? Why's that?"

"Well, I've seen Jess around—and I've watched who he hangs out with. He doesn't seem like the kind of guy who's into drugs."

The older officer shrugged. "Who knows? All that counts is that we found this in his bed. He can try to deny that it's his, but there's no getting around the facts."

Jess did deny it. He swore that he knew nothing about the "stuff." The young officer, recognizing that they had the guy "cold," decided to open the guy up since he is so persistent in his innocence:

Young Officer:	You seem awfully upset about this situation.
Jess:	You bet I am! These guys have been trying to get me to push this stuff for months and when I refused, they decided to set me up to teach me a lesson!

Officer: So you're saying that they set you up because you wouldn't go along.

Jess: That's it. It's no alibi. If you check it out with some of the other street people, they'll back me up.

Officer: Who could I talk with who might know?

Jess: Artie, the guy who cleans up at the Mexican joint over on Palmer Street could run it down to you. Be cool though, and don't put him on Front Street.

Officer: So, this Artie could give us some information?

Jess: Right!

Officer: OK. I'll check this all out. In the meantime, though, I'll have to book you until we see how it all washes out.

SKILLS MAKE THE DIFFERENCE
Well it did "wash out"; Jess was telling the truth and it was verified. Larry was picked up and eventually provided the officers with useful information about some of the transactions on the street and was able to name some names.

The use of skills here really had a payoff. But just what is communication all about? We know that some officers can really talk with people and others cannot.

Why It's Important to Communicate
Although you see and hear it all the time, chances are you are never really sure what is really going on inside another person. At the most fundamental level, people are all human beings and, probably, much more alike than different, even though it is obvious that criminals are not the same as law enforcement officers. The gulf between you and other people may often be

Understanding Means Effectiveness	frustrating. In one way you feel that you know a person, but in another way, you are sure you do not. And knowing other people is important at times. The better your understanding of another person, the more effective you can be in terms of managing him.
Communication Promotes Understanding	This is where communication skills become important add-ons. When you choose to use these skills, you can find out a great deal more about where individuals are. You can add to your understanding and action in ways that will help you defuse tension, decrease the chances of trouble, and increase your ability to handle any and all situations more effectively. The basic skills covered in Section I let you size up the situation. The add-on communication skills presented in this section let you understand the full implications of that situation and act constructively.
WHAT ARE THE SKILLS?	Once you choose to communicate, you begin by putting all of the four basic skills to use: positioning, posturing, observing, and listening. As the process of communicating develops, you use new skills in two important ways.
The Two Skills	• Responding to People
	• Asking Relevant Questions
	As the materials that follow make clear, responding to people means a good deal more than just answering a greeting—although this, too, can be important. You need to take the initiative in developing effective responses. By the same token, asking relevant questions means more than a simple "Hey, what's going on?" Here in Section II, you will have a chance to learn the specific procedures involved in responding and asking questions effectively.

As noted, communicating must begin with your use of all the basic skills. You position yourself at the best possible distance—say three to four feet away—when you are talking with a single person (although this would certainly increase if you sized up danger). This puts you close enough to see and hear everything, yet not so close that you seem overly threatening. You face the individual squarely, your left shoulder squared with his right and your right with his left. And you look directly at him, making appropriate eye contact to let him know you're really "right there."

You position yourself to communicate both confidence and real attention. You observe the appearance and behavior, using visual cues to draw inferences about feelings, the relationship with you, and general energy level. You listen carefully, making sure you take in all the key words and verbal indications of intensity so that you can determine just what a person's need really is. Only after you have really mastered and put to use the basic skills will you be able to use the add-on communication skills effectively.

Like the basic skills, communication skills involve a step-by-step approach. First you respond to the person. Next you ask any relevant questions you need to ask. Then you respond again, this time to their answers. You would usually not, in other words, just jump in and start asking questions—at least not if your goal is to get the person to open up and communicate useful information voluntarily. There may be times when the circumstances warrant using more intimidating tactics. However, we do not have to teach intimidation, and intimidation always contains significant risk.

Think of officers you have worked with who were better at communicating than other officers. What qualities or skills did these good communicators have that made them effective? List two.

_____

_____

_____

_____

Responding

Responding means just that—showing a clear reaction to something that you have seen or heard. A response **gives evidence** that you have listened. In this section, we will take a look at several levels of responding. At the simplest level, you can respond to content by summarizing and expressing what a person or group of persons has said or done. At the next level, you can respond to the feelings shown in a person's words or reflected in his actions, particular feelings, and the reasons for those feelings.

There are three levels of responding:

INTERVENTION
MODEL

THE ADD-ONS

Communicating with People

Ask Questions

Respond

1. Responding to content
2. Responding to feeling
3. Responding to feeling and meaning

Each new level of responding does more to show a person that you are really on top of things—really seeing, hearing, and understanding him or her in terms of where he or she is. Probably more than anything else in this training, responding is going to seem strange to you. It is new and you may be doubtful about its worth. There are some things to remember here:

1. We are not telling you that you cannot use other communications techniques that have worked for you in the past.

43

2. We are trying to "add on" to techniques you may already have to increase your communication abilities.

3. The more techniques you have to handle a given situation in life, the greater your chances of success or control of the outcome. Techniques are like tools in a toolbox: the more you have and know how to use them, the greater chance you can fix a problem.

Responding to content. Responding to content is the skill of seeing and hearing what is really happening and the ability to reflect that understanding back to a person. You are letting a person know that you heard them accurately and are on top of the situation.

There are two steps to responding to content: a) reflecting on what was seen and heard, and b) using the responding format to respond to content.

Ask Questions

Respond

1. Responding to content
   a) Reflect on what was seen and heard
   b) Use responding format to respond to content

Responding skills add to what you already do rather than necessarily replace what you do. The more responses you have to **choose from**, the more effective you can be. By practicing responding, you will not only learn it, but also learn the best places and ways to use it. You cannot choose a skill from a skills repertoire that you do not have.

44

While your use of the basic skills establishes a relationship in which people are more likely to cooperate with and talk to you, responding is a tool you can use spontaneously to communicate with anyone. Responding to content is the first part of effective responding. It shows a person that you have heard or seen what he or she said or did. When any person, including those you must manage, knows that you are seeing and/or hearing him or her accurately, he or she will tend to talk more freely. This is critical because talking not only gives you more of the information you need, it also allows people to get things off their chest.

RESPONDING at the simplest
level reflects content:

"You're saying _____."

Use the Basics

When responding to content, you are focused on what people are either saying or doing. Using what you have learned, you focus by posturing and positioning yourself for observing and/or listening to the person.

Reflect on What Was Seen and Heard

Next, you reflect on what you have seen and heard: "What is he doing?," "What is he saying?" and "How does he look?" In answering these questions, stick close to what is actually going on and/or what is being said.

Use Responding Format

Finally, after taking it all in and reflecting on it, you summarize what the people are saying or doing in your own words. You respond to the content by saying to a person either:

"You look (it looks) _____" or

"You're saying _____."

For example: "You **look** pretty busy" or "You're **saying you're** pretty busy."

45

You respond to content when you want more information to aid you in management. You may do this when you are interrogating someone, or when you notice unusual behavior in a person or group of persons and would like to get some information from them about what they are doing. For example, you might notice a group of unusually talkative guys being very quiet. You could say to them: "You guys seem pretty quiet today." This gives them the opportunity to respond to you while also letting them know that you are observing them and observing them accurately. Unlike other approaches designed to get information, responding to content does not automatically put people on the defensive.

PRACTICE   List two examples of situations in which you might respond to content in order to get more information.

1. _____

2. _____

List two reasons why you might want to get involved with another person.

1. _____

2. _____

Get People to Talk Instead of Act!   People can sometimes experience anxiety when they encounter law enforcement personnel. Of course, if you are the one who summons assistance, your anxiety will most likely decrease upon the law enforcement officer's arrival. You can be driving along the highway and observe an officer managing someone else's routine traffic violation and your anxiety increases. You will glance at the speedometer and probably let up on the gas pedal, even if you are within limits. As a law enforcement officer, you should recognize that you are a significant person in society and that average citizens are threatened by the perceived consequences of an encounter with you.

When managing people who have anxiety and when you have sized up that no real danger exists, it is a good idea to let people talk off some of their anxiety rather than have them act it out. Responding will assist greatly in accomplishing this.

Example   Here is an example: You have successfully separated a feuding couple. They do not appear to be affected by drugs or alcohol. You choose to both reduce their intensity and to find out what the general problem is. You position yourself so that you are not vulnerable and also so that you can listen, observe, and respond. You instruct the couple on your ground rules. Only one person talks at a time! The female speaks first, "He threatens to beat me up every time we run out of money! He thinks I squander it somehow! God knows I can barely put food on the table, such as it is, and he blames me because he ain't got no decent work!"

You respond to her content: "You're saying he blames you for the money running out when the way you see it there just isn't enough for basic things." This response reflects some understanding of the way **she** sees the situation. It is non-judgmental and encourages further talk (better than screaming or attacking the husband or you). Responding to content as you did is a valid response. It helps defuse the situation.

Person	Officer	Group
1) Gives the setting. **2)** Role plays.	**1)** Attends. **2)** Waits 30 seconds. **3)** Gives responses: "You're saying _____." "You look (it looks) _____."	**1)** Positions, observes, listens. **2)** Writes own response. **3)** Rates officer's response. "Yes," if accurate, "No," if not, plus reason. **4)** Rates officer's attending.

**PART 2 OF
RESPONDING**

Responding to feeling. Responding to feeling is the ability to capture in words the specific feeling experience being presented by a person. By responding to, or reflecting back, the person's feeling, you show that you understand that feeling. This encourages the person to talk—to release his or her feelings.

The two steps in responding to feeling are: a) reflect on feeling and intensity, and b) respond to that feeling.

Ask Questions

Respond

1. Responding to content
2. Responding to feeling
    a) Reflect on feeling and intensity
    b) Respond to feeling

Every person has feelings that affect what they say and do. The nature and strength of these feelings usually determine what a person is going to do. When you respond to a person's feeling, you are encouraging him or her to talk. The skill of responding to feelings has important implications for the management of people.

RESPONDING at the next level
reflects feelings:

"You feel _____."

Understanding Can Defuse Bad Feelings

Showing that you understand how a person feels can be more powerful than showing that you understand the content of his actions and/or words. Showing a person that you understand his negative feelings can usually **defuse** those negative feelings. By responding to feelings at the verbal or "symbolic" behavior level, you keep the person's words from turning to action. Also, responding to feelings at a verbal level can give you the necessary clues to determine the person's intention. If he clams up after you have responded to his feelings, he may be telling you that he is going to act on them; on the other hand, if he acknowledges your response verbally, he is telling you that he wants to talk it out instead of act on it. You all know the difference between a talking fight where the parties are looking for a way out ("Yeah" versus "Oh, yeah!") and a real fight where the fists will be flying any second.

Greater Understanding

Besides being able to defuse negative feelings so that words do not become negative actions, responding to feelings leads to greater understanding of, and by, a person. A person cannot always link up his feelings with the situation and is often at a loss to understand where he is. In addition, when you respond to positive feelings, these, feelings get reinforced (unlike negative feelings). There is nothing mysterious about this. We do not enjoy our negative feelings, so we get rid of them by sharing them—by talking them out. But we do enjoy our positive feelings, so they only become stronger when they are shared with another person. You can choose to strengthen the positive feelings that will help a person act more positively simply by recognizing and responding to these feelings. As a general rule, a person who feels positive about him- or herself will try to do positive things, while a person who feels negative about him- or herself will try to do negative things. If you expand on this, you arrive at the general principle: People tend to act in ways consistent with the way other significant people see and act toward them.

If you put together a person's low self-image and the fact that others have a low image of him as well, you can predict that the person will act accordingly (negatively). Now you cannot pretend that a man is positive when he is not, but if in fact he feels positive or does something that is positive, then recognizing this will help.

PRACTICE List two situations where it would be important and useful to defuse negative feelings.

1. _____

_____

2. _____

_____

Use the Basics For responding to feeling, you position and posture yourself, then observe and listen. Then you reflect for the feeling (happy, angry, sad, scared) and its intensity (high, medium, or low).

Finally, you respond by saying:

"You feel _____ ."

For example, "You feel angry."

Reflect on Feelings

Happy?
Angry?
Sad?
Scared?
Confused?

Here, the new skill involves reflecting for feeling and intensity. Adding a new skill does not mean discarding the old skills, of course. When reflecting for feeling, you are really asking yourself, "Given what I see and hear, how does this person basically feel?" Is he happy, angry, sad, scared, or confused? The person's behavior and words will let you make a good guess at the feeling. For example, an individual who shouts at another person, "You stupid idiot, now look what you've done!" while he shakes his fist and gets red in the face is obviously feeling a level of anger.

Reflect on Intensity of Feelings

High?
Medium?
Low?

After you have picked out the feeling word, you must reflect on the intensity of the feeling. For example, anger can be high in intensity (boiling mad), medium in intensity (frustrated), or low in intensity (concern). The more accurate your feeling word reflects the intensity, the more effective your response will be. That is, your response will be more accurate and will do the job better (e.g., defuse the negative feeling). You would not choose *concerned* for the above example because the term is too weak to describe a man yelling, shaking his fist, and turning red. Such an understatement would probably only make him more angry, but "You feel furious" would fit fine.

Take each of the five basic feeling words (happy, angry, confused, sad, and scared) and write a high, medium, and low intensity word for each.

FEELING WORDS

	High	Medium	Low
Happy	_____	_____	_____
Angry	_____	_____	_____
Confused	_____	_____	_____
Sad	_____	_____	_____
Scared	_____	_____	_____

ROLE-PLAY ACTIVITY

Officer Communicator	Officer Responder	Group
1) Shares a real* problem. **2)** Rates response after group rating.	**1)** Positions, observes, listens. **2)** Pauses 10 to 20 seconds. **3)** States, "You feel _____."	**1)** Positions, observes, listens. **2)** Writes own response: "You feel _____." **3)** Rates "Yes/No" on officer's response and tells why. **4)** Gives individual response to group.

*Should not be anything that would be intimidating, embarrassing, or hurtful to self or others.

Responding to feeling and meaning. Responding to feeling and meaning combines the two previous skills. It requires you to paraphrase the content of a person's statement in such a way as to provide a meaningful reason for the person's feeling.

The two steps in responding to feeling and meaning are a) reflect on the feeling and the reason for that feeling and b) respond to the feeling and meaning.

Ask Questions

Respond

1. Responding to content
2. Responding to feeling
3. Responding to feeling and meaning
    a) Reflect on feeling and reason
    b) Respond to feeling and meaning

Reflect on Feeling and Reason

Learning how to respond to content and how to respond to feeling has prepared you to respond to feeling and meaning. Now your response at this new level can put everything together. Here you will effectively capture where the person is at the moment. By adding the meaning to the feeling, you will help yourself and the person to understand the reason for his or her feelings about the situation. The reason for this is simply the personal meaning for the person about what is happening.

53

Example For example, a fellow officer in danger of being pulled into a fight when his record is clean and a promotion is coming up might feel "afraid" because "the fight could blow my chances to get promoted." The personal meaning of the potential fight for this officer is that it might blow his chances for promotion. He is not afraid of fighting, but rather of not getting the promotion.

RESPONDING at the highest level reflects both feeling and meaning.

"You feel _____ because _____."

By putting together the feeling and meaning and responding to both, you show a person that you understand his experience as he presents it. This increases the chances of the person talking to you about the thing in which you are interested. In addition, for interrogation purposes, you will be able to learn more about what the person values and what bothers him so that you can understand him and, if necessary, use this information to apply pressure on him. For example, one officer might be confronted with a hostile citizen who is refusing to be searched.

Citizen: No way. You're not going to search me just because some lady told you some crap. I don't have anything you'd be interested in: Go bother some rapist and quit bothering me!

Officer: You feel angry at me because you don't understand why this is necessary. In a situation like this, we just can't take chances; it's our procedure.

54

Citizen: Well, it's embarrassing; it's like I'm a damn criminal.

Officer: I'm sorry about that but it just has to be done. (And he does.)

The officer is responsive to the citizen because he chooses to be. He believes it will—in both the short- and long-term—have a better impact. Note that he does it while continuing to carry out his duty. He avoids "machismo" to keep the intensity manageable.

In another situation, a citizen discusses a concern he has about his teenage son:

Citizen: He's headed for trouble. I just can't control him any more. All he listens to are the punks he runs with.

Officer: You feel worried because you know that unless your son wakes up he's going to be just like them.

Citizen: Yeah. They are into dope and none of them work. You know what's going to happen when you see that.

Officer: You feel kinda scared because you can see how the dope problem leads to other problems for kids.

Citizen: Right, and it's getting worse, all the time, and I don't know what to do.

Officer: Is he in school?

Citizen: Yeah, he goes to the voc-tech school downtown.

The officer understands clearly where the citizen is in the situation and where he wants (or needs) to be. This became possible because the officer was able to attach an understanding of meaning to the feelings of the citizen.

Respond to Feeling and Meaning By building on what you know, you add the reason to the feeling response you have just learned. Your new way of responding becomes "You feel _____ because _____."

What we need to focus on here, of course, is an individual's reason (personal meaning) for his or her feeling. Supplying the reason means that you must understand why what happened is important. You do this by rephrasing the content in your own words to capture that importance. You are actually giving the reason for the feeling. In this way, you make the person's feeling clearer and more understandable.

It is also important to capture whether the person is seeing him- or herself as being responsible or seeing someone else as responsible. Your response should reflect where he or she sees the responsibility in the beginning, even though you may not agree. By doing this, you will have a better chance of getting the person to open up. You can always disagree when it becomes necessary and effective to do so. Remember, if you have this skill, you can choose to use it. If you do not have it, you have no choice.

PRACTICE A person has been a "snitch" for a particular officer until the day the person suspected that word had leaked out about his activities. He confronted the officer, his eyes narrowed and his hands trembling.

"You rotten fink! You promised you wouldn't rat! Now they know about me. You really screwed me over!"

Identify the intensity and category of this feeling and pick an accurate "feeling" word to describe the person's emotion.

Feeling Word: _____

Now supply the reason for the person's feeling. What does his situation really mean to him? Who is he blaming? Why is all of this so important to him? To understand what's going on, you have to forget that you may not have leaked anything; forget that you had your reasons if you did tell someone; ignore the seeming personal attack. What does this mean to him? Put yourself in his place. Recognizing the meaning, formulate a response.

Response to Feeling and Meaning:

"You feel _____ because _____

_____

_____ " .

The officer who was actually involved knew how to initiate communication with a person in a tense situation like this, and he recognized that failure to do so could mean real trouble. He knew that the person's basic feeling was anger. He knew that the intensity of this feeling was high and that the person was really furious. And he knew that the person was blaming him for risking his life—the real meaning of the situation for the person.

Knowing all of this, the officer was able to respond effectively to the feeling and to what this feeling meant: "You feel furious because I put your life in danger." This response caught the person flat-footed. He had expected the officer to deny everything—to tell him to shut his mouth and to ignore the whole thing. He certainly had not expected the officer to respond to his situation at the same level that he was experiencing it!

Because the officer knew how to respond at this level, he was able to keep the person talking openly. And in a tense situation, this can mean the difference between effective management and genuine danger!

Referral When responding to feeling and meaning, a communication interchange may sometimes go deeper than you feel you can handle. If this happens, you must consider the option of a **referral**. With your added understanding, your referral will be that much more specific and beneficial.

But many times, your added understanding will provide you with the information you need to really manage people. The payoff for you will be rewarding. Many officers put in their time, but do not get the payoff because they lack some of the skills needed to finish off the good start that they make by being decent and fair. Responding is one way to ensure the payoff.

Practice your responding skills with persons with whom you have been communicating. When you practice the skill, do not just give one response and say to yourself, "Well, I did it." Keep using your responding skills over and over again when you choose to understand. When you feel someone has said all they are going to say, or when you know all you need to know, then you can take action.

But be careful about giving advice or getting involved. A lot of times, a person will hold back until he or she sees how you react. If you tell the person what to do or become overly involved, you may be placing yourself in either a vulnerable situation or one over your head.

ROLE-PLAY ACTIVITY

Officer Communicator	Officer Responder	Group
1) Gives real stimulus. **2)** Gives spontaneous reply following each response. **3)** Rates responder after group rating.	**1)** Positions, observes, listens. **2)** Pauses 10 to 20 seconds. **3)** Gives response: "You feel _____." **4)** Pauses 10 to 20 seconds. **5)** Gives response: "You feel _____ because _____."	**1)** Positions, observes, listens. **2)** Writes down own response to feeling and meaning. **3)** Rates "Yes/No" on last response. If no, why? **4)** Gives individual response to group. **5)** Gives feedback on sizing up.

Asking Questions

While you ask questions in order to get useful answers, some questions get better answers than others: the skill of asking questions will help you increase your information base and, hence, your ability to manage others.

The two steps in asking questions are:

THE ADD-ONS

Communicating with People

Ask Questions

1. Using the 5WH method
2. Reflecting on answers and recycling

Respond

As the following materials make clear, there are really two basic steps involved in asking relevant questions in an effective way. First, having responded to a person at the most accurate level, you must develop one or more questions of the 5WH type: Who, What, Where, When, Why, and How. Second, you must **reflect** on the answer or answers given by the person to make sure you fully understand all the implications. Did you get the information you wanted? Was new information revealed?

Asking questions will help you manage. If people answered our questions satisfactorily, we would be all set. After all, we have all the right questions. The reality, however, is that for a variety of reasons (e.g., lack of trust, guilt), many people do not answer questions fully or accurately. In fact, questions will sometimes have the opposite effect. That is, they will shut off communication with people rather than open it up. This is because questions are often seen as the bullets of the enemy ("Cover up, here they come"). The only way questions can be really effective in getting a person to open up is when they are used **in addition to** the basic skills plus responding. Use of the basics plus responding can get a person to the point where he or she will talk quite openly. It is at this point that questions can make their contribution by getting some of the necessary specifics (who, what, when, where, why, and how—the 5WH system).

Use the Basics Plus Responding

STEP 1 OF ASKING QUESTIONS

Asking 5WH questions. Answers to questions will give you the detail you need to manage people effectively. The more details you know, the better you can understand what is going on. You always want to know *who* is involved, *what* they are doing or going to do, *when* and *where* something happened or will happen, *how* it is going to be done or how it was done, and *why* it did or will take place.

"Where were you?"
"Who were you with?"
"Why were you there?"
"What did you actually do?"
"When did all this happen?"
"How was it handled?"

Respond, Then Ask

When you have all this information, you can take appropriate action and/or prevent problems from happening (now and maybe in the future). Question-asking can be used with responding during an interrogation, interview, or when you choose to assist with a problem.

Responding opens up the person and gives you a chance to make sure you understand what is being said. It also builds up trust with a person. For these reasons, you should always try to respond to a person's actions or words at the highest possible level before you actually start asking questions. Questions then fill in the details of the picture. Often, details (reasons) can come from responding skills alone, if you have patience. If they do not, questions are appropriate. It is as simple as that.

PRACTICE For each of the following situations, first make a response and then ask an appropriate question.

1. You are actively looking for a suspect in a case. You are questioning a young man known to be the suspect's friend. You observe that the young man has on some expensive clothes and jewelry that you infer are out of this person's price range since you know he is unemployed. You inquire, and the young may says:

"Jesus, man, can't a guy buy some things without being persecuted? I used my own savings to buy these things and I've been saving for quite a while, too. You just don't believe anybody. A guy can't even take care of himself. Why don't you find something else to do besides hassling me?"

Respond: "You feel _____

because _____

_____ . "

Questions (5WH): " _____

_____ ?"

2. A person admits to you: *"I know I'm stuck on the stuff. I know it's killing me."*

Respond: " _____

_____ ."

Questions (5WH): " _____

_____ ?"

3. A young man who, at one time was a troublemaker, confides the following to you:

"That vocational school is really great. I tuned my first car the other day. The instructor said it was a perfect job. Thought I'd let you know."

Respond: " _____

_____ ."

Questions (5WH): " _____

_____ ?"

PART 2 OF ASKING QUESTIONS

Reflecting on answers to questions. It is not enough just to ask good questions. You also have to be able to make sense out of the answers you get (and also recognize the answers you are still not getting). Begin by responding to the answer: "You're saying _____" or "So you feel _____." Then *reflect* on or think carefully about the answer to your question.

The person may be leveling with you and giving you the information you need to manage things or even to provide assistance. This person may be leveling with you as best he or she can, but perhaps not giving you all the information you need. Or this person may be covering up something, which means that he or she is still not fully open—still not really communicating with you. Your *observation* skills are critical here.

REFLECTING means thinking about what
you have—and have not—learned.

How does he look?

What is he doing?

What did he say?

What didn't he say?

Recycling

When reflecting on the person's answer to your question, you can think about four specific things: How does he look as he answers (relaxed, uncomfortable); what is he doing while he answers (facing you and making eye contact, looking away, looking down at his feet); what he has actually said (the information content of his answer); and what he may have failed to say (any "gaps" in the way he answers). By reflecting on these four areas of concern, you can make sure that you fully understand all the implications of the answer. Once you have responded to this answer, you can ask additional questions to get the rest of the information you need. By using your basics—responding, asking good questions, reflecting, and then responding again—you will be recycling.

Example

Let us imagine that you are talking with a young ex-con who has not been out of prison too long. You have recognized that he is really scared stiff because of the pressure he is getting from some group on the street. And you have been able to respond to him at the level of feeling and meaning: "So, you really feel scared because these guys just want to take you right over." Now you are set to ask a question: "Who are the guys who have been hassling you the most?" The ex-con looks around quickly, then down at his feet. When his answer comes, it is given in a low, unclear voice: "Oh, just some of the guys from the old neighborhood."

You look at his appearance and see he is really uptight. He will not look you in the eye—he will not even speak up in a clear voice. On top of this, he's answered your questions with only the vaguest kind of information. In the end, his answer gives you nothing.

Upon reflection, you realize that the guy is not only scared in general, but is really frightened right now, like he does not want to be seen talking to you. In other words, your reflecting lets you know that this is not a guy who is trying to play it smart with you. He is not clamming up on purpose. Instead, he is just living in fear, right there in front of you.

Realizing all of this, you are able to respond even more fully and immediately to him: "You're scared stiff right now because whoever's hassling you might get wind of us talking together." And the ex-con looks up, surprised. He did not know any officer could really see and hear him as he actually is. You have just grown about six inches in his eyes—maybe to the point where you suddenly seem stronger than the threat of those who have been hassling him! Instead of clamming up, the young man keeps on talking, answering your next questions more fully. This is just what you wanted him to do, because in the end, you know you gained his confidence and learned the information you needed to get.

ROLE-PLAY ACTIVITY

Person	Officer	Group
1) Role plays stimulus.	**1)** Positions, observes, listens.	**1)** Positions, observes, listens.
2) Reacts to responses and answers questions.	**2)** Pauses and responds to feeling and/or meaning.	**2)** Writes own responses and questions.
3) Gives feedback.	**3)** Asks questions after responding (5WH).	**3)** Rates officer's response.
	4) Pauses and reflects on answer to question.	**4)** Rates question "Yes/No."
		5) Presents each response and question.
		6) Gives feedback on sizing up.
		7) Reflects on choice of response: Would it have warranted both feeling and meaning?

Summary of the Add-Ons

Jimmy was an inmate who everyone—officers and other inmates alike—invariably referred to as "a bad mother." There was a lot of respect in this phrase. You learned respect around Jimmy. How could you help it? He was 6 feet 5 inches, 275 pounds, and a former sergeant in the Green Berets. To top it off, he had a temper like a bear just coming out of hibernation who found the ground was still frozen solid.

Jimmy did not like officers. In his time, he had sent more than a few to the hospital. By now, the officers had figured out a drill. When they wanted Jimmy out of his cell, six of them went in and brought him out. Even then it was not easy. He just naturally loved to crack heads. A "bad mother" indeed!

One day a new officer who had been on the street came on to begin his duty at the jail. The old hands were happy to show him around. "Listen," they said. "You gotta meet Jimmy."

"Jimmy?" The new guy did not have a whole lot of experience on the job, but he knew a set-up when he saw one. "Who's he? What's his story?" Half a dozen seasoned officers accompanied the new man to Jimmy's cell, grinning and nudging each other. Oh, they would not let the new guy get hurt or anything. But it sure would be something to see his face when Jimmy tried to crush his head like a grapefruit!

"Hey, Jimmy—you got someone to see you," one of the officers told the huge inmate, unlocking the cell and moving back quickly.

Jimmy's only answer was a grunt. He had been sleeping. Now he emerged slowly from his bunk scowling and rubbing his eyes.

"What do you miserable creeps want now? Man, I'm gonna tear somebody into small pieces if you come close enough!" His eyes focused on the new guy for the first time. "What's this, some kinda bait or somethin'?"

The experienced officers expected the new guy to back off when he saw Jimmy towering over him. Instead, the new man stuck out his hand.

"I'm Ben," he said. "I guess you're really ripped at us for just barging in on you."

The other officers saw Jimmy's brow furrow. He had been about to swing and they had been all tensed up to jump in. But now Jimmy seemed unsure. He did not shake. But he also did not swing.

Then his face cleared. In another moment he flung his head back and laughed out loud. "Whooeee!" He calmed down at last and looked at the new guy. "I knew it! I knew if I just hung around this place long enough, they'd have to send in a real human being to handle me!"

And that was it. In choosing to initiate communication instead of using force, the new officer had taken Jimmy off guard. This was a new approach. More than that, it was an indication to an inmate full of anger and hostility that maybe there still were people out there who could talk to him—even listen to him. And that knowledge made all the difference in the world to Jimmy.

What enabled the new officer to make this kind of difference, of course, was his communication skills—in particular, responding. And these are the same skills you yourself have begun to master.

In the first section of this manual, you learned the skills you need to size up a situation. Now, working through this second section, you have learned the skills you need in order to initiate meaningful communication to improve your management potential—the skills involved in responding and asking questions. These skills are designed to help you manage by using communication skills. The payoffs are always good for all concerned. Now it is time to move on—to go beyond sizing up and communicating—and consider what is involved in really controlling the situation. We will concentrate on this topic and the skills it requires in the final section of this manual.

THE APPLICATIONS

Controlling Behavior

THE ADD-ONS

Communicating
with People

THE BASICS

Sizing Up the
Situation

Section III

The Applications:
Controlling Behavior

The application skills combine the basic and the add-on skills, and are aimed at controlling behavior. These skills are important in helping you maintain control and manage people well.

The applications include three specific skills:

INTERVENTION
MODEL

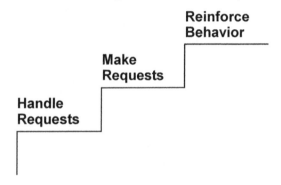

APPLICATIONS

Controlling Behavior

An officer who had been on the force for a few years really resented one of his regular assignments. He had to "baby sit" a bunch of snot-nosed kids who hung out at the shopping center—a bunch of spoiled brats. As a kid, he worked all the way through high school. He did not play ball or belong to clubs—nothing like these kids who all had silver spoons in their mouths. He pretty much resented them. As a result, he ran a tight ship: every wheel had better be perfectly adjusted and those mufflers had better muffle.

Every now and then, he just scattered kids for being a nuisance. They were all up to no good anyway. He believed that if he made life miserable enough for them, they might learn to appreciate what the words *law* and, especially, *order* meant.

The kids resented back. Letters to the editor of the local newspaper questioned the kids' "harassment." He laughed it off. The chief was no friend of the newspaper anyway. One evening, he was sitting quietly in his patrol car at the shopping center. He watched the seemingly endless parade of kids cruise around the fast food restaurant in the shiny cars their parents had sacrificed to give them. From a few yards away, he heard some loud shouting and banging. He got out and carefully checked to see that all doors were secure. He had already radioed in so that the dispatcher would know where he was and what he was doing.

As he approached the area of the noise, he observed that several kids were wildly waiving their arms. Some appeared to be wrestling, but as yet, no bodies were on the pavement. "What the hell's going on here?" He shouted his question to get attention; there was command presence in his voice.

The gathering of youths quieted some. One young man whom he had already identified as one of the leaders shouted back at him. "Our girls' basketball team just won the regional tournament. Wanna lock us up for inciting a riot?" He shrugged and returned to his patrol car. Smart aleck kid. Should have chewed his butt for being so disrespectful. Ah, screw 'em. As he pulled out, he noticed people at the entrance to the mall laughing and pointing at his car. "What the hell?" He put on his light, opened the door, and got out. Tied to his rear bumper was the split rail fence belonging to the taco shop in the shopping center; he had dragged it almost out of the mall.

This is just one of hundreds of stories that make a similar point: not all the ways in which officers try to manage people are good. Some are actually dangerous, more than a few have proved disastrous, and some are just aggravating. Many ineffective methods of control have been based on the myths and folktales passed down through many generations of law enforcement workers. The problem with the majority of these is that they treat anything other than a show of pure force as a sign of official weakness. Yet the fear of looking weak in peoples' eyes has actually caused many officers to mismanage people—like the officer in the above story.

One thing is certain: as soon as an officer begins to develop effective interpersonal management skills, he begins to experience the real reward of being able to control situations with less tension, less force, a lot less risk to himself, and with less hassle.

But let us go back to the story for a moment. There are a number of things the officer could have done to avoid getting into the situation he forced himself into.

For one thing, he could have consistently used the basic sizing up the situation skills we covered in Section I. By using these skills—and especially those involving observation and listening—he would have had a far more complete understanding of the situation among the kids. Even more importantly, of course, he could have responded to them. This more than anything else would have let them know—in constructive rather than antagonistic terms—that he was really aware of each and every one of them. Yet even effective use of basic skills plus use of communicating skills does not guarantee results. This officer, like every officer, needed specific yet constructive ways of managing people in his job. This section of the manual will outline a number of such ways—the "applications" that any officer should have open to him or her.

Controlling Is the Key! Controlling behavior simply means taking charge. This is what it's all about in law enforcement. Without the ability to control behavior, all the other efforts are wasted. An officer has to do everything he or she can to ensure appropriate behavior: in the interests of society, in him- or herself, and of individuals. The same holds true for all of us. Learning to control our behavior is in our interest. Without control, nothing productive can or will occur.

This section of the manual builds on previous sections. It is about the *hows* of controlling behavior by using good management skills.

WHAT ARE THE SKILLS? In this final section of the manual, we will take a close look at three different areas of skills. These skills are dealt with here as applications, because they really represent the specific ways in which you can apply all of the other skills you have developed in order to manage and control behavior in the most effective possible manner.

Three Application Skills
- Handling Requests
- Making Requests
- Reinforcing Behavior

Unlike the earlier skills in Sections I and II, these three areas are not all cumulative—that is, you will be involved at any given time in either handling requests or making requests of your own. In either situation, however, you will want to reinforce the behavior—positively if you want someone to keep doing a particular thing, and negatively if you want to keep him from doing something.

Before going any further, let us take a look at a couple of these skills in action.

Here is a routine situation where an officer dem-
onstrates skill in management. It could be handled
much differently with more negative outcomes. It
involves both the law enforcement officer making
a request and, in turn, a request being returned to
the officer.

Sgt.: Larry, I'd like you to switch your shift
with Paul for the next two weeks
because Paul has been having
problems with his neck and can't ride.

Officer: Is it okay with you if I try to get someone else to do it? I'd like to keep my
schedule as it is since I started bowling
in a league.

Sgt.: I'm sorry, Larry, I know that would upset
your schedule, but I can't use anyone
else since you are the only one who
can switch in your unit. I've already
checked it out with the other guys. It will
only be until Paul's neck gets better or
we transfer him.

Officer: Why do you always pick on me? I'm
always the one who gets screwed on
these deals.

Sgt.: I know this irritates the hell out of you
because it will interrupt your routine, but
it's the best I can do right now. Please
report at 10:00 a.m. tomorrow instead
of 2:00 p.m.

Control through Skill The sergeant in this case used his skills to control his situation. He did not demean or put down, and he did not use sarcasm. You will observe, however, that included in his skills were firmness and reasons for his actions. There was no weakness. The officer now knows what he is expected to do and why. The sergeant was even able to continue to be responsive to the officer when the officer became irritated. The use of skill gets the job done and increases the probability that the officer will feel he has been treated fairly, even if he has to have his routine interrupted.

PRACTICE Why is control important for management?

_____

_____

_____

What does an officer gain when he learns to control his own behavior?

_____

_____

_____

Handling Requests

Handling requests is the ability to manage requests in a fair and effective manner. The skillful handling of requests helps build trust and reduce tension.

The two steps in handling requests are:

INTERVENTION
MODEL

APPLICATIONS

Controlling Behavior

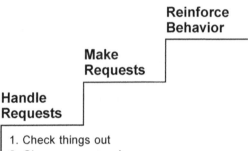

1. Check things out
2. Give response and reason

RULES, REGULATIONS AND RIGHTS

Before we turn to the skills involved in handling requests, we should review the way in which rules and regulations often relate to the specific things to which people do and do not have a right.

Although times are changing rapidly, each officer is bound by certain legal and departmental requirements to provide certain things to society. Most of these things are seen to be basic rights and/or needs to which all citizens are entitled. You, as an officer, probably have written regulations to guide you in these areas. Abiding by these rights and needs usually enables an officer to establish a working relationship with most everyone.

There is always that 10 to 20 percent who react negatively no matter what you do. But by following the regulations, you can fairly expect people to do what is expected. You have taken away excuses for negative behavior, even in the eyes of the people who want to see you as the aggressor and the citizen as the victim. When you attend effectively to people, you have fulfilled your basic obligations to manage people within the law.

You can either attend as the result of a person's request or by initiating on the basis of some need you see. The latter really gets a person to open up. (As used here, *attending* really refers to both of the skills we will consider—checking the person out and responding to his or her request with a reason for your decision.)

PART 1 OF HANDLING REQUESTS

Checking out the person and situation. It goes without saying that you, as an officer, are and will be receiving requests from people. Some will be legitimate, some not. Each request must be responded to. Even if you ignore a request, you have responded to it, and some consequence will occur that can affect your ability to handle and control people. If you find this hard to believe, put yourself in a situation where you want your shift supervisor to consider one of your own requests and he ignores you. How do you feel? What message would it communicate if it happened often? What might be the consequences of it on your behavior?

Use Basic Skills

Know Rules and Regulations

CHECKING OUT REQUESTS involves
deciding if they are legitimate or not.

78

Before you respond to any request, you need to use your basic skills to check out the person who makes it. Is this person leveling with you, or is he or she trying to play some kind of game? You also need to check out the situation in terms of any policies or regulations that might apply. Using your positioning, observing, listening, and responding skills will be invaluable to you here. As you practice, this will become very clear to you.

PRACTICE Read the following situations, then describe how you would check them out.

A citizen approaches you and makes this request:

Citizen request: "Officer Smith, can I just leave my car here? This place has been out of business for a month. No one will be unloading here."

What skills would be important to use in this situation?

_____

_____

What rules or regulations must be considered?

_____

_____

Another citizen makes this request five minutes before you go off duty:

Citizen request: "Officer Smith, would you come over to my apartment house? There's this kid over here who doesn't look too good. I think his parents are abusing him."

79

What skills would be important to use in this situation?

_____

_____

What rules or regulations must be considered?

_____

_____

By knowing which of the sizing-up and communicating skills to use, you can ensure that you really know what is happening with a particular person who has a request. And by reviewing the appropriate rules and regulations, you will have a good idea of whether the request is or is not legitimate. Now you are ready to respond to the request itself.

PART 2 OF **Responding with a reason for your decision.**
HANDLING This skill involves indicating the action you are
REQUESTS going to take—your decision—and giving the person your reason. Giving the person a good reason is not a sign of weakness. On the contrary, it is the best way in which to minimize future gripes. If you turn the person down, he or she will not be able to complain that you did not even say why. And if you grant this person's request, he or she will know that it was just for this one situation and for a good and clear reason.

RESPONDING with a reason
eliminates possible hassles.

Reasons for Action	Basically, an officer has three possible avenues of action in relation to a request. In each case, the officer should give some reason for his or her action. Here are some formats that can be used:

"Yes"	"Yes, I'll do (it) _____ because _____."
"No"	"No, I won't do (it) _____ because _____."
"I'll check"	"I'll look into (it) _____ because _____."

How You Decide	In each instance, the officer bases his or her intent on the laws and the regulations. In cases where people need or request something beyond what they are entitled to by law and regulation, each person's behavior (past and present), what is asked for, the way it is asked for, and the information you have gained by checking things out should determine your response. For example, an individual might ask you, "Hey, man, how about a lift?" "No, I can't allow you to have a ride. It's against the department's policy to give rides to anyone. Sorry."

Take Care of Basic Rights	While an officer may have an option in a case like the above, some things—like responding to citizens in distress—cannot be denied. You may have options for an abusive citizen who demands attention, but you cannot deny him emergency service that is warranted. Knowing the law and the regulations of your department will definitely make your job easier. By taking care of the basic rights of citizens, tensions will be greatly reduced.

Taking care of basic rights is a must in any relationship. It would be very hard for a citizen to believe you wanted to assist him if you did not attend to his basic rights—that is, if you did not give him what he was entitled to. Dealing with such needs in a concrete way builds up trust that will make it more likely that you will get the trust and support you and your department wants from the public.

List four legitimate requests citizens could make:

1. _____

2. _____

3. _____

4. _____

List four non-legitimate requests citizens could make:

	Request	Why
1.	_____	_____
2.	_____	_____
3.	_____	_____
4.	_____	_____

ROLE-PLAY ACTIVITY

Citizen	Officer	Group
1) Gives the setting. **2)** Makes request. **3)** Gives feedback after group has finished their assignment.	**1)** Positions, observes, listens. **2)** Checks things out. **3)** Pauses 30 seconds to assess request (legitimate or not). **4)** Gives action plus reason.	**1)** Positions, observes, listens. **2)** Checks things out. **3)** Rates officer: a) action plus reason; "Yes/No"; b) action and reason; if no, why? _____ **4)** Gives action plus response for feedback.

Making Requests

Making requests is the ability to manage people by making specific requests of them. Making requests skillfully improves the chances that they will cooperate and more readily carry out your requests.

The two steps in making requests are:

APPLICATIONS

Controlling Behavior

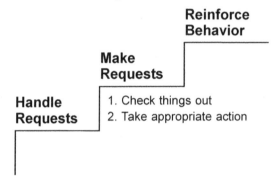

The two procedures involved in making requests in an effective way are checking things out (using the same procedures as when you are handling requests) and taking appropriate action. As before, you need to check things out to ensure that you do not make the wrong move—a move that might increase tension rather than calm things down. Once you have done this, you can decide whether the best action will involve a simple request, an order, or even direct physical action.

Check things out. Since the procedures here will be the same as those involved in handling requests, there is no need to go back over them at length. Here, however, your aim should be to understand as much as possible about the situation involving the person who you plan to have do something: Is he with his friends? If so, what is his probable relationship to them? Will he feel he is losing face if you give him an order and therefore react antagonistically? By using your basic sizing up and responding skills, if there is any tension in the air, you can make sure that whatever action you take in making your request will be effective.

Know the Situation

Use Basic Skills

CHECKING THINGS OUT involves the use of your basic and responding skills.

Take appropriate action. Making requests of people is obviously a routine part of law enforcement. Many requests are made each shift, and often little thought is given to the impact of requests both on the control of persons and their immediate and long-term cooperation. Yet, it is how the request is made that often makes the difference, not the nature of the request.

TAKING ACTION means selecting the best way to make your request.

How You Ask May Mean More Than What You Ask

In taking action to get a person to do something, you will remember that you have to be specific. You should identify what you want done and when. Telling a person in this manner keeps you clean. You have put it right out there for him or her, and anybody else, to see. Many officers have found a polite request is effective in getting a person to do what he is told.

Of course, there are officers who feel that people do not deserve politeness, or that being polite makes an officer look weak. But you were brought up with good manners, and the question is, are you going to let a person who is not being polite bring you down to his level? In addition, when a person does not do something reasonable when asked politely, then it is he who looks weak and not you. Moreover, by being initially polite, you have given the person the opportunity to go "the easy way." Now it is his responsibility if you have to go "the hard way."

Mild or Polite Format

It may be difficult to use a polite format, but many officers have found that it is more effective to be polite. It gets the results you want. A mild (polite) request can take the form "Would you (please) _____?" or it can take the form "I would appreciate it if you would _____." When you make a request, the most direct method is simply to identify what you desire, and then use the format "I want you to _____." But because people often resent authority if you are simply telling them to do something, you may have fewer hassles if you use more of a request format. Examples might be "I'd like you to do _____" or "Would you stop _____?"

Direct Format

Softening a Request

You can soften the statement even more by using polite words: for example, "I'd like you to *please* stop _____." What format you use for making a request will depend on the situation and the particular person. Of course, if a person abuses the mild method, you are always free to move to a stronger position, including a direct order. As indicated above, the point is to get the job done—to have the person do what you want. Most experienced officers agree that over time, it is generally better if direct confrontation can be avoided.

Get Stronger When Necessary

You may also want to use your responding skills in taking action. For example, you come across a person who is in a place where he should not be. You *position* yourself so that you can see him, but he cannot see you. You *observe* for a little while because he appears to be doing nothing else wrong. Then you move into *position* so that he can also see you. You approach cautiously—he may be armed. As you approach, you recognize the person. He makes no sudden moves. In fact, he gives you a greeting: "Hello, Officer." You give him the benefit of the doubt in the sense that you are open to what he is going to say. The person is a new individual to the area and you have not seen or heard anything to make you more than routinely cautious. You make your request:

Officer: Hi! This is a posted area. You'll have to leave it right now.

Person: I just wanted to get off by myself for a while.

Officer (softening by responding):   I can appreciate your wanting some privacy but you'll have to leave right now.

PRACTICE There may be times when you want to start right out with a direct order or take immediate action. List two examples when you would give a direct order or take immediate action without making a request. Give the reason why you would do this.

Direct Order:

Situation 1: _____

_____

Situation 2: _____

_____

Take Immediate Action:

Situation 1: _____

_____

Situation 2: _____

_____

ROLE-PLAY ACTIVITY

Person	Officer	Group
1) Gives the setting. **2)** Role plays inappropriate behavior.	**1)** Leaves room. **2)** Enters and uses basic skills during 30-second pause, then makes request.	**1)** Positions, observes, listens. **2)** Records own version of request and why it should be made. **3)** Rates officer: "Yes/ No" on content and style of request, then gives own version of request.

Reinforcing Behavior

Reinforcing behavior means attaching or withdrawing something pleasant associated with a behavior. Punishment means associating unpleasant consequences with a behavior.

The three steps of reinforcing behavior are:

APPLICATIONS

Controlling Behavior

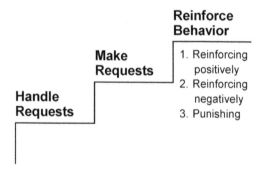

The only reason people finally do anything is because of the consequences (positive or negative) of doing it or not doing it. Behaviors only change when there are consequences. There are clearly examples of persons being **rewarded** for **inappropriate** (bad) behavior. Criminals who go uncaught are reinforced by the attention and material gain. Whining children are given sweets to quiet them in grocery stores. Police officers may receive the adulation of their peers for their expression of force.

Using rewards and punishment appropriately can have both short-term and long-term positive influence in law enforcement. It can enhance the likelihood of responsible behavior from persons immediately and also assist in more long-term outcomes, such as citizen cooperation and support.

Two Kinds of Reinforcement   You can use yourself as a reinforcer by giving **verbal** and **nonverbal** approval to persons for behaviors you believe warrant reinforcing. You can demonstrate disapproval of behaviors by not approving of their behaviors. To do so, you must either have established a relationship (rapport) with the person, so that your approval means something, or you must develop consequences for persons that take away certain privileges. If you express verbal or nonverbal approval or disapproval to a person and there is no rapport, your attempt to reinforce by removing a privilege or desired condition that is not perceived as positive by a person will have little or no intended effect.

REINFORCING means using positive and negative rewards verbally and nonverbally.

Verbal   Verbal reinforcement means expressing orally something you know is pleasantly experienced by a person and associating it with some positive, responsible behavior: "Bob, thank you for always being prompt with your report," or "Bob, I appreciated you taking the responsibility for that without being asked."

Nonverbal   Nonverbal reinforcement means adding the reinforcement without using words. The most obvious **Positive Reinforcement** would be smiling, nodding the head, etc. A person who moves his vehicle to provide a larger space for better pedestrian movement and gets a nod and a smile from an officer is an example of positive nonverbal reinforcement.

Negative Reinforcement   A parolee you know hangs out at a local pub, a violation of the conditions of his parole (which you have overlooked). You hear from a reliable source that he has started a ruckus or two after having a **Punishment** few too many drinks. You confront him about it and tell him he can no longer have that privilege.

PRACTICE You give a citation to a citizen for an infraction. You know that a judge will assess a fine of at least one hundred dollars. This, in addition to the inconvenience of having to appear in court, is a punishment. List some negative reinforcers and the behaviors that would warrant them.

Negative reinforcers:

1. _____
2. _____
3. _____
4. _____

Behaviors receiving them:

1. _____
2. _____
3. _____
4. _____

List some punishments you can administer and the behaviors that would receive them.

Punishments you might give:

1. _____
2. _____
3. _____
4. _____

Behaviors receiving them:

1. _____
2. _____
3. _____
4. _____

List some positive reinforcers you can administer and the behaviors that would warrant them.

Rewards you might give:

1. _____
2. _____
3. _____
4. _____

Behaviors you might reward:

1. _____
2. _____
3. _____
4. _____

ROLE-PLAY ACTIVITY

Citizen	Officer	Group
1) Gives the setting and trust level in existence. **2)** Role plays. **3)** Reacts to officer's responses. **4)** Gives feedback.	**1)** Responds, observes, listens. **2)** Responds. **3)** Reinforces: a) "If you do not, then___." b) "If you do, then___." c) "Since you are___, then ___." d) "Since you are not___, then___." **4)** Gives some personal verbal reinforcement (positive or negative).	**1)** Positions, observes, listens. **2)** Writes own reinforcement and why. **3)** Rates officer: "Yes/ No" on correctness of reinforcement. If "No," why? **4)** Gives responses for feedback. **5)** Rates use of basics.

Summary of the Applications

You have developed professional skills to do a professional's job. You have helped to lay to rest that familiar stereotype that "civilians" have of the law enforcement officer as a brutal, brainless machine that delights in getting people locked up. And you have gone beyond and begun to act upon one of the most basic equations in all of human history.

HUMAN ACTIONS DETERMINE HUMAN REACTIONS The cornerstone of the interpersonal management skills you have learned is **decency:** simple human decency. You have a job to do. But in doing it, you have learned how you can handle people like the human beings they are. And in return, you will be able to promote more decent and constructive behavior on their part. This process involves what has been called "the principle of reciprocal behavior"—a fancy way of saying that **we all get back what we give.** In your case, you have learned how to invest your work with professional effectiveness—with real skills—and still give people decent treatment.

References

Charles, L. L. (2007). Disarming people with words: Strategies of interactional communication that crisis (hostage) negotiatiors share with systemic clinicians. *Journal of Marital & Family Therapy.* (33), pp. 51-68.

Johnson, R. R. (2007). Race and police reliance on suspicious non-verbal cues. *Policing.* (30), pp. 277-287.

Lau, E. Y. Y., Li, E. K. W., Mak, C. W. Y., & Chung, I. C. P. (2004). Effectiveness of conflict management training for traffic police officers in Hong Kong. *International Journal of Police Science and Management.* (6), pp. 97-109.

Morris, M. W., Leung, K. & Iyengar, S. S. (2004). Person perception in the heat of conflict: Negative trait attributions affect procedural preferences and account for situation and cultural differences. *Asian Journal of Social Psychology.* (7), pp. 127-147.

Novaco, R. W. (1977). A stress inoculation approach to anger management in the training of law enforcement officers. *American Journal of Community Psychology.* (5), pp. 327-346.

Syeed-Miller, N. (2006). Developing appropriate dispute resolution systems for law enforcement and community relations: The Pasadena case study. *Ohio State Journal on Dispute Resolution.* (22:1), pp. 83-103.

Tyler, T. R., Lind, E. A., & Huo, Y. J. (2000). Cultural values and authority relations. *Pscyhology, Public Policy, and Law.* (6), pp. 1138-1163.

Vecchi, G. M., Van Hasselt, V. B., & Romano, S. J. (2005). Crisis (hostage) negotiation: Current strategies and issues in high-risk conflict resolution. *Aggression & Violent Behavior.* (10), pp. 533-551.

Wilson, C. & Brewer, N. (1993). Individuals and groups dealing with conflict: Findings from police on patrol. *Basic and Applied Pscyhology.* (14), pp. 55-67.

About the Author

Steve J. Sampson, Ph.D.
Founder, President

Dr. Steve Sampson has been teaching conflict resolution and interpersonal skills for over 30 years. He brings both academic knowledge and practical experience to his seminars.

As an Educator, he holds a Bachelors Degree in Sociology from the University of Massachusetts (1970) and a Masters (1976) and Doctoral Degree (1981) in Counseling Psychology from Georgia State University. He is a nationally recognized Master Trainer in Interpersonal Communication Skills since 1977, and has presented that training to over 300 agencies and organizations in 40 states. He is a former Assistant Professor of Criminal Justice at Georgia State University from 1979 to 1985. More recently, he retired from his position as a Clinical Professor in the Counseling and Psychological Services department at Georgia State University (1995-2004).

As a Licensed Psychologist, he is the former Chief of Psychology of Georgia Regional Hospital, Atlanta, Georgia (1993 to 1995). He is also a nationally recognized counseling psychologist who works with various law enforcement agencies conducting fitness for duty evaluations and post shooting debriefings since 1982. He has been a contract Psychologist with 25 Metropolitan Atlanta Law Enforcement Agencies since 1991.

As a Criminologist, Dr. Sampson is the former correctional superintendent for Massachusetts Halfway Houses Inc. (1969 to 1973), as well as the former Correctional Superintendent for the Georgia Department of Corrections (1974 to 1976). He has provided training to over 250 prisons, law enforcement, and public safety agencies in Social Skills Training since 1977.

As an author, he has published the following books on Social Intelligence Skills:

- *Social Intelligence Skills for Law Enforcement Managers*
- *Social Intelligence Skills for Correctional Managers*
- *Social Intelligence Skills for Government Managers*

He has recently published a new book:

- *How to be in a Personal Relationship*

Made in the USA
Las Vegas, NV
08 December 2021